Love is a Beautiful Thing

$\mathcal{F}$or

LOVE IS A
Beautiful
THING

COMPILED BY
ESTHER BEILENSON

DESIGNED BY
KERREN BARBAS

PETER PAUPER PRESS, INC.
WHITE PLAINS, NEW YORK

For Larry—
You complete me.

Text copyright © 2000
Peter Pauper Press, Inc.
202 Mamaroneck Avenue
White Plains, NY 10601
All rights reserved
ISBN 0-88088-110-0
Printed in China
7 6 5 4 3 2 1

Love Is A *Beautiful* Thing

$\mathcal{Y}$ou cannot explain
why two people love
each other or find each other.
It's something that either
works or it doesn't, and you
certainly don't want
to mess around with it
when it's working.
LEA THOMPSON

$\mathcal{T}$he success of my show
is great, losing weight is great,
but nothing compares
with being in love.
OPRAH WINFREY

*L*ove is a fire. But whether it is going to warm your hearth or burn down your house, you can never tell.

JOAN CRAWFORD

I don't think you can look for love. All you can do is get yourself in a situation when you don't discourage something that may be rather nice.

LINDA RONDSTADT

Love is
inseparable
from knowledge.
ST. MACARIUS OF EGYPT

*W*hat I know now
is that being in love
is not enough.
A relationship needs
nurturing, and if you
neglect it, it falls apart.
It's hard to taste all the
sweet stuff in life if you
don't have people you love
to share it with.
LEEZA GIBBONS

*L*ove may not make the
world go 'round, but it
makes the ride worthwhile.
FRANKLIN P. JONES

*I*f you really want it to
work in a relationship, you
have to meet in the middle.
It's not coach and player.
It's a team.
JULIA ROBERTS

*L*ove is friendship
set on fire.
JEREMY TAYLOR

*L*ove has nothing to do
with what you are expecting
to get — only with what you
are expecting to give —
which is everything.
KATHARINE HEPBURN

*T*he one I trust
is the one I love.
BILL COSBY

*P*eople who throw kisses
are hopelessly lazy.
BOB HOPE

*O*ur fights are huge,
but our love is huge.
PATRICK SWAYZE

[*L*ove] changes everything.
LAUREN BACALL

*I*f you can make the girl
of your dreams laugh a lot,
she'll fall for you.
CARROLL O'CONNOR

*L*ove is the only gold.
ALFRED, LORD TENNYSON

*T*each only love
for that is what you are.
A COURSE IN MIRACLES

*L*ove is a force
more formidable
than any other.
It is invisible —
it cannot be seen
or measured, yet
it is powerful enough
to transform you in a
moment, and offer you
more joy than any
material possession could.
BARBARA DE ANGELIS

Love is
the river of life
in the world.
HENRY WARD BEECHER

Honor
the ocean of love.
GEORGE DE BENNEVILLE

You can give
without loving,
but you cannot love
without giving.
AMY CARMICHAEL

All mankind
loves a lover.
RALPH WALDO EMERSON

It's not
just the good times
that matter. It's the
not-so-good too. That's
no reason to not want
to be with someone you love.
It's a reason to stay. It's a
reason to love him and to
want to be there.
WHITNEY HOUSTON

$\mathcal{L}$ove is not
a matter of
counting the years—
it's making
the years count.
WOLFMAN JACK

$\mathcal{L}$ove does not consist
in gazing at each other
but in looking
outward together in
the same direction.
ANTOINE DE SAINT-EXUPÉRY

$\mathcal{L}$ove laughs
at locksmiths.
PROVERB

*A successful marriage
requires falling in love
many times, always
with the same person.*
MIGNON MCLAUGHLIN

*In the coldest February,
as in every other month
in every other year,
the best thing to hold
on to in this world
is each other.*
LINDA ELLERBEE

*I*n our life
there is a single color,
as on an artist's palette,
which provides the meaning
of life and art.
It is the color of love.
MARC CHAGALL

I love the sense
of play that we have.
And for me, facing
the world together
and having this
wonderful, solid base.
KELLY PRESTON

Gravitation
is not responsible
for people falling in love.
ALBERT EINSTEIN

People think
love is an emotion.
Love is good sense.
KEN KESEY

Love is but the discovery
of ourselves in others,
and the delight in the
recognition.
ALEXANDER SMITH

*W*here there is
great love, there are
always wishes.
WILLA CATHER

*Y*ou will find
as you look back
upon your life that the
moments when you
have truly lived are the
moments when
you have done things
in the spirit of love.
HENRY DRUMMOND

*Y*ou, yourself,
as much as anybody
in the entire universe,
deserve your love
and affection.
BUDDHA

*I*n love
the paradox occurs
that two beings become one
and yet remain two.
ERICH FROMM

*L*ove takes off
masks that we fear
we cannot
live without and
now we cannot
live within.
JAMES BALDWIN

*Y*ou can wish
you were in love,
but you have to wait
until the object
of your affection
knocks on your door.
ANJELICA HUSTON

I have learned
not to worry about love,
but to honor its coming
with all my heart.
ALICE WALKER

*I*t was total love
at first sight.
There was this big
empty white room,
and she (Rebecca Romijn)
walked in. It was like a
dopey, romantic movie.
Everything
was in slow motion.
JOHN STAMOS

If you fall in love
and it doesn't work out,
you get a broken heart.
What comes out of that
will make you a better lover
and partner the next time.
GRIFFIN DUNNE

It's a whole other mode —
you thought you knew
what loving was like,
and you suddenly realize
you had no idea.
JAMES BROLIN

*W*e stood there
in silence, looking into
each other's eyes
and smiling. A flash of
recognition zapped us—
a deep reciprocal
awareness....We both
understood we would be
together for the rest
of our lives.
MARILU HENNER

*I*t takes courage to love.
ANONYMOUS

*W*e are not
held back by the love
we didn't receive
in the past, but by
the love we're not
extending in the present.
MARIANNE WILLIAMSON

*W*hat a grand thing,
to be loved! What a grander
thing still, to love!
VICTOR HUGO

*W*e are most alive
when we're in love.
JOHN UPDIKE

*L*ike all true values,
love cannot be bought.
HERMAN HESSE

I like not only
to be loved,
but to be told
I am loved.
GEORGE ELIOT

Love is like a violin.
The music may stop
now and then, but the
strings remain forever.
JUNE MASTERS BACHER

With love
it's better to live
even the simple,
ordinary day.
JAN NOHA

*L*ove is not
a matter of counting
the years,
it's making
the years count.
W. SMITH

*T*o love and be loved
is to feel the sun
from both sides.
DAVID VISCOTT

*P*rayer is not optional.
Neither is love.
HEBREW PROVERB

*L*ove is a
ticklish sensation
around the heart.
WELSH PROVERB

*W*hat shall I do to love?
Believe.
What shall I do to believe?
Love.
IRISH PROVERB

*I*f you have
love in your life
it can make up
for a great many things
that are missing.
If you don't have love
in your life, no matter
what else there is,
it's not enough.
ANN LANDERS

*T*o love means
you also trust.
JOAN BAEZ

Love is
all new, fresh.
MICHAEL DRURY

There are
some people
who have the quality
of richness and joy
in them and they
communicate to
everything they touch.
It is first of all
a physical quality,
then it is a quality
of the spirit.
THOMAS WOLFE

$\mathcal{L}$ove in action
is the answer
to every problem
in our lives and in this
world. Love in action
is the force that helped
us make it to this place,
and it's the truth that
will set you free.
SUSAN TAYLOR

$\mathcal{R}$omance is the icing
but love is the cake.
AUTHOR UNKNOWN

*O*ne is very crazy
when in love.
SIGMUND FREUD

*L*ove is the greatest
refreshment in life.
PABLO PICASSO

*T*he first duty of love
is to listen.
PAUL TILLICH

*A*ll, everything that I
understand, I understand
only because I love.
LEO TOLSTOY

*D*o what you love.
Know your own bone;
gnaw at it, bury it, unearth
it, and gnaw it still.
HENRY DAVID THOREAU

We've got this gift
of love, but love is
like a precious plant.
You can't just accept it
and leave it in the
cupboard or just think
it's going to get on by itself.
You've got to keep
watering it. You've got to
really look after it
and nurture it.
JOHN LENNON

When you love
someone all your
saved-up wishes
start coming out.
ELIZABETH BOWEN

Can there be a love
which does not make
demands on its object?
CONFUCIUS

I did not just fall in love.
I made a parachute jump.
ZORA NEALE HURSTON

I did not know
I loved you until I heard
myself telling you so.
For one instant I thought,
"Good God, what have I
said?" and then I knew
it was true.

BERTRAND RUSSELL

*T*hey do not love
that do not show their love.

WILLIAM SHAKESPEARE

To fall
in love is easy,
even to remain in it
is not difficult; our
human loneliness
is cause enough.
But is a hard quest
worth making to find
a comrade through whose
steady presence
one becomes steadily
the person one
desires to be?
ANNA STRONG

*L*ove is a canvas
furnished by Nature
and embroidered
by imagination.
VOLTAIRE

*W*e come to love
not by finding
a perfect person,
but by learning to see
an imperfect person
perfectly.
ANONYMOUS

*L*ove is like pi —
natural, irrational,
and very important.
LISA HOFFMAN

*T*his is the miracle
that happens every time
to those who really love;
the more they give,
the more they possess.
RAINER MARIA RILKE

*T*o love someone
deeply gives you
strength.
Being loved
by someone
deeply gives you
courage.
LAO-TZU

*T*rouble is a part
of your life, and if you
don't share it, you
don't give the person
that loves you
enough chance
to love you enough.
DINAH SHORE

*E*veryone admits
that love is wonderful
and necessary, yet no one
agrees on just what it is.
DIANE ACKERMAN

*I*n a great romance,
each person plays a part
the other really likes.
ELIZABETH ASHLEY

*L*ove is a great beautifier.
LOUISA MAY ALCOTT

*L*ove is
a chain of love
as nature is a chain of life.
TRUMAN CAPOTE

*L*ove is a verb.
CLARE BOOTHE LUCE

*L*ove is a friendship
set to music.
E. JOSEPH COSSMAN

*F*alling out of love
is chiefly a matter
of *forgetting* how
charming someone is.
IRIS MURDOCH

*W*hen a love affair
ends it may take
a while to see
what's grown in its stead,
but usually it's you.
MINNIE DRIVER

Loving
can cost a lot
but not loving
always costs more,
and those who fear
to love often find
that want of love
is an emptiness
that robs the joy
from life.
MERLE SHAIN

Those who love
deeply never grow old.
ANONYMOUS

*W*e waste time looking for
the perfect lover, instead of
creating the perfect love.
TOM ROBBINS

*T*he magic of first love is
our ignorance that it can
ever end.
BENJAMIN DISRAELI

*W*e were friends first, and
then the love thing came
around second, and that's
how it still is.
JADA PINKETT,
ON HUSBAND, WILL SMITH

*W*icked men obey from fear; good men, from love.
ARISTOTLE

*Y*ou can't put a price tag on love, but you can on all its accessories.
MELANIE CLARK

*T*reasure the love you receive above all. It will survive long after your gold and good health have vanished.
OG MANDINO

If you wish
to be loved, love!
SENECA

It's easy
to halve the potato
where there's love.
IRISH PROVERB

We love because it's the
only true adventure.
NIKKI GIOVANNI

*L*ove in its essence
is spiritual fire.
EMANUEL SWEDENBORG

*W*e don't need
to limit our concept
of love.
KEVIN COSTNER

*I*t is not
so much true that all the
world loves a lover
as a lover loves
all the world.
RUTH RENDELL

Love is the only thing
that keeps me sane.
SUE TOWNSEND

Love is as strict as acting.
If you want to love somebody,
stand there and do it.
If you don't, don't.
There are no other choices.
TYNE DALY

Love is a fruit
in season at all times.
MOTHER TERESA

Love is
an irresistible desire
to be irresistibly desired.
ROBERT FROST

Nothing
is too much
trouble for love.
DESMOND TUTU

The sanest thing
in this world is love.
ANNE SEXTON

To a loving person,
everybody is worthy
of love, every occasion
an opportunity
to practice love.
EKHATH EASWARAN

Love —
or else the lack of love —
is felt so deeply
by all of us.
MEG RYAN

[Y]ou have
to remember what
matters most: which is
giving real, balanced,
caring, unconditional love.
MERYL STREEP

The heart
has its reasons
that reason does not know.
PASCAL

*W*here love
is concerned,
too much is not
even enough.
PIERRE DE BEAUMARCHAIS

*B*lessed is
the influence of one true,
loving human soul
on another.
GEORGE ELIOT

*S*oul meets soul
on lovers' lips.
PERCY BYSSHE SHELLEY

*T*he more
I think about it,
the more I realize
there is nothing
more artistic
than to love others.
VINCENT VAN GOGH

Love is a Beautiful thing Lo
utiful thing Love is a Be
ing Love is a Beautiful
e is a Beautiful thing Lo
utiful thing Love is a Be
ing Love is a Beautiful
e is a Beautiful thing Lo
utiful thing Love is a Be
ing Love is a Beautiful
e is a Beautiful thing Lo
utiful thing Love is a Be
ing Love is a Beautiful
e is a Beautiful thing Lo